Mary Miraculous

Mary Miraculous

Extraordinary Stories of Ordinary People
Touched by Our Lady

Tom Sheridan

ASSISTING CHRISTIANS TO ACT
PUBLICATIONS

Mary Miraculous:
Extraordinary Stories of Ordinary People
Touched by Our Lady
by Tom Sheridan

Edited by Gregory F. Augustine Pierce
Cover Design by Tom A. Wright
Typesetting by Garrison Publications

Published by ACTA Publications
             Assisting Christians To Act
             4848 N. Clark Street
             Chicago, IL 60640
             800-397-2282

Library of Congress Catalog number: 97-77685
ISBN: 0-87946-176-4
Printed in the United States of America
02 01 00 99 98 5 4 3 2 1 First Printing

Contents

Introduction

Mary is news. Some 2,000 years after the biblical events in which she played a critical role, the Mother of God is still today appearing on the covers of weekly newsmagazines and the pages of daily newspapers. She's even turning up on TV news reports, in novels, movies, plays and videos.

This should not be surprising. Mary has always attracted the attention of skeptics and captured the hearts of believers.

Perhaps it's because this courageous, holy, loving woman seems so approachable, so under- standing, so compassionate. Throughout the ages, faithful Christians have believed they have seen her face and heard her voice all over the world. The Roman Catholic Church has taken those appear- ances seriously enough that seven of them—includ- ing those of Guadalupe, Mexico, in 1531; Lourdes, France, in 1858; and Fatima, Portugal, in 1917— have been approved as "official."

Just in the last decades of the 20th century, hundreds—even thousands—of personal encounters with Our Lady have provided revelations of her message of peace and love. Believers have experi- enced Mary's presence at Medjugorje in the former Yugoslavia and elsewhere around the world, both in very public, media-covered apparitions and in very private, unreported prayers and conversations.

The miracle is in the eyes of the beholders for Marian appearances such as these. For the Church, belief in direct communication with Mary can be acceptable, unless the message is in conflict with Scripture or Tradition. Official or not, most people who experience such events come away with a renewed appreciation of Mary's call for hope and repentance.

In the summer of 1997, for example, a rough, working-class neighborhood in the Chicago suburb of Hanover Park was the scene—for those who saw it—of a miracle of Mary. High on the brick wall of an apartment building, a shadow in the shape of the Madonna became visible only after nighttime security lights were turned on. Hundreds and hundreds of believers gathered, and many wondered why Mary would choose to show up there.

One woman said, "I think she's making an appearance to show the world that it's not over, that we should live in peace and harmony."

That's a common Marian theme. In Clearwater, Florida, an image on the tinted windows of an office building attracted the attention of believers in 1996. Clearly visible in the two-story vision was a head, hooded robe and torso. The image shimmered in green and blue and red, said observers.

"It was like you're in an angel's arms and the light of Christ was above and around you," said a Florida woman who watched from across the street.

Skeptics, of course, claim there are natural causes for apparitions such as these—and there may well be. But for believers, there clearly is something mystical and mysterious going on. And though the Church does not recognize these as "official" encounters with the Mother of God, the message most of her followers discern—to believe, to pray, to act for others—is certainly consistent with the teachings of the Church.

Devotion to the woman in the Bible whom we know only as Mary, the espoused of Joseph and the mother of Jesus, is as ancient as Christian history. According to the Gospels of both Luke and Matthew, salvation began with Mary's radical act of trust—her cry of "yes" to the will of God as recorded in her immortal Magnificat:

> *My soul magnifies the Lord and my spirit rejoices in God my Savior, for he has looked with favor on the lowliness of his servant. Surely, from now on all generations will call me blessed, for the Mighty One has done great things for me and holy is his name.*
>
> *Luke 1:46-49*

Mary was the first believer in Jesus' mission. She has been called "the perfect disciple." More than anything else, that distinction flows from the special connection between mother and child. It is clear from the Scriptures that Mary was among the first followers of Jesus, was faithful even at the foot of the cross, and was among the disciples at Pentecost. Somehow she knew from the beginning that her son was the Savior, the Messiah, the Holy One of God. That is the core of the Magnificat. That is the essence of her intervention in the miracle at Cana. That is what is meant when Mary ponders her role as the mother of the child Jesus after he is found in the Temple.

In Catholic tradition, Mary—the immaculately conceived child-woman, the virgin mother, the Mother of God—is revered as "Queen of All Saints." Yet she remains one of us: a human being, woman, daughter, wife, mother, widow. Because she clearly experienced the challenges of everyday life—the joys and sorrows, the hopes and disappointments, the struggles and successes—Mary seems to many people a gracious guide, a maternal mentor, a compassionate companion. Thus she has become for millions a conduit, a channel, a mediatrix of grace, and the focus and intercessor of prayer.

This special recognition of Mary has never been far from the heart of the Church. Even when devotion to Our Lady has been overdone by some indi-

viduals or groups, the Church has remained remark-
ably constant in its interest in and teachings about
Mary. Today there is a definite resurgence of aware-
ness of Mary's special relationship with Jesus, which
remains the center of traditional Church teaching
about Mary.

Mary's place of honor is a long-standing tradition from the earliest moments of the Christian
community as it assembled to remember and celebrate Jesus. It was at the Council of Ephesus in the
year 431 that the Church solidified its understanding
of Mary's place in the Christian faith. The council
debated, rejected challenges to the uniqueness of
her role, and agreed that Mary should bear the
revered title "Mother of God." It is a singular honor.

In the centuries and generations that followed,
devotion to Mary prospered, even as some of the
more excessive devotional practices have waned.
The Second Vatican Council, more than 1,500 years
after the historic agreement at Ephesus, was pur-
posely opened on the Feast of Mary, the Mother of
God. Pope John XXIII recognized that Mary's role in
the Church remains that of mother and model of
faith, hope and love.

In many quarters of the Church, there is a
renewed spirit of that recognition. The rosary and
novenas to Our Lady are becoming popular once
again; pilgrims still journey to Guadalupe, Lourdes,
Fatima, and other places of Mary's appearances

recognized by the Church. Thousands more flock to the sites of other reported apparitions—scenes of inspiring and faith-filled, though not official, encounters with Our Lady.

The Church recognizes—and permits—such private revelation. While these do not carry the seal of the Church, for those who have experienced them they are a powerful witness of the presence of God. But for most believers, there is no need for an actual vision of Mary. Rather, people experience in the course of their ordinary daily lives a sense of Mary's presence, of her strength, of her desire for peace.

Technically, we know we do not pray to Mary but rather ask her to intercede for us with God. She is blessed, but not worshiped; honored for her role in the life of her son, but not divine herself. Still, she is for each of us an example of how the power of God can—when we proclaim our own "yes"—burst into our lives.

Those who come face to face with Mary—whether in prayer or in a personal revelation—are likely to uncover in the depths of their being a greater sense of love, a more focused spiritual life, and a concern for others that becomes vitally important. Encounters, apparitions and visions of Mary that do not call us to a greater love of God and for all humankind—the love that Mary herself has—must be fraudulent. Those who follow them are doomed to

draw away from, not closer to—as Mary herself
would certainly have us do—the spirit of Jesus.

This book is filled with small miracles in which
God indeed bursts into the lives of people through
the intercession of Mary. In these stories, Mary is the
connection to God's power and presence. The
people who tell the stories are aware of, understand
and believe in Mary's place in their life and faith.

The entries included here were among thousands told by people who answered my simple
request to share their miracles of the touch of God in
their lives. I wrote letters to the editors of newspapers in Catholic dioceses all around the United
States and Canada. I also sent notices to hundreds
of parishes asking them to include my request in
their bulletins. (This invitation is repeated for the
reader on page 93 of this book.)

Responses poured in from more than 40 states
and at least two foreign countries. Many of the
miracle stories people recounted included their
experiences with Mary or her rosary. It is these
stories that this book shares.

A miracle may not be so much what happens to
us, but whether or not we see in what happens to us
the hand of God. These are personal miracles, told

by the faithful for the faithful. They exist as examples of faith meant to lead others to that faith.

It was interesting to note, in letter after letter, a common phrase. It usually went something like this: "I saw your letter and felt compelled to write...." Note the word *compelled.* It was used over and over.

Some people see miracles all around them every day. Others are caught up short when faced with an apparently miraculous event, skeptical yet finally willing and able to see it. Others barge through life, never really understanding the powers that swirl around them and never seeing all there is to see. This book is for all three groups, but especially the last.

All miracles are a call to rediscover the sacred in our lives. Mary is the model for this kind of holiness, and so we can call her "Miraculous Mary." The Mother of God is news today because people hunger for the miracle she is.

A Rule of Life for Those Consecrated to Mary

Remember that you belong exclusively, unconditionally, absolutely, irrevocably to the Immaculate. Whoever you are, whatever you have or can, whatever you do (thoughts, words, actions) and endure (pleasant, unpleasant, indifferent things) belong to the Immaculate. Consequently, may she dispose of them according to her will (and not yours).

You are an instrument in her hand, therefore do only what she wants; accept everything like children from their mothers; trust her in everything.

When you pray, pray thus: O Immaculate, my life (every moment of it), my death (where, when and how) and my eternity belong totally to you.

—St. Maximilian Mary Kolbe

Our Lady of Good Counsel

*Mary, Mother of Our Lord and
Our Lady of Good Counsel,
throughout the ages of faith
you have been a source of hope
and welcome guidance.*

*Speak to us, your people who long
for words of advice,
direction and encouragement.*

Help us to always seek you.

*We ask this through Jesus,
your Son, our Lord.
Amen.*

"I Didn't Know What to Do"

The morning began like most others when I was a young college student. I walked across the old town of Annapolis, Maryland, from the campus of St. John's College to St. Mary's Church. I was just in time for the 7 a.m. Mass.

Strangers are not hard to spot at daily Mass, and the woman who entered the pew in front of me was not a regular. She was bent over or crippled. During Mass, she just sat there, not participating, not receiving communion.

The thought struck me that I should pray with this woman for a healing to her back, but the idea was foreign to me. Who was I to pray with a stranger? With these feelings flooding my spirit, I followed her out of church after the service. Just as we reached the vestibule, I reached out my hand and touched her shoulder.

I was about to say something like, "May I pray with you?" But before I could get the words out, she turned, fell into my arms, and began to weep.

I didn't know what to do. Here I was, a shy college student standing in the back of a church with a strange woman crying in my arms. All I could do was pray silently, trusting in God to guide me.

The woman soon calmed down. She told me her daughter had run away several days earlier.

That's when I realized the woman didn't have a physical problem. Rather, she was bent over with grief.

I caught sight of an icon of Our Lady of Perpetual Help on the wall of the chapel. So I told the woman that Mary would understand her sorrow. After all, her own son had "run away" to the Temple when he was 12 years old. Together we prayed the *Hail, Mary*.

The woman told me she had come to church seeking a priest for consolation. I found the priest who celebrated the Mass, but he spent only a few moments with her. It was the police department's job to find her daughter, he said.

So I offered to return with the woman to the police station to see if they had learned anything. At the station there was no news of her daughter. While we were waiting, my gaze wandered to a photo on a bulletin board, though at the time I didn't pay much attention to it. I gave the woman my phone number and she drove me back to campus.

Later in the day, I was giving a campus tour for the college's admissions office. In a library reading room, I saw someone who seemed familiar. Startled, I thought, "It's the woman from church," but it wasn't. Then I realized, "It could be her runaway daughter." I had recognized the young woman from the photo on the bulletin board at the police station, even though I hadn't known it was of her.

After the tour, I rushed back to the library. The girl was still there. I thought perhaps I could persuade her to call home. Finally though, I just contacted the police. That was the right thing to do. The police were very gentle. The daughter went home with them.

Later that evening, the mother called me to ask if I had anything to do with her daughter's homecoming. I told her the whole story. Then I remembered the icon of Mary in the church and realized the adventure had happened on the Feast of the Visitation.

—David, Walla Walla, Washington

Glorious Mysteries, Glorious Help

What some others might consider a small miracle, I consider a big one.

I have had a long career as a consultant on warehousing and distribution. More than 40 years ago, I responded to an ill friend's plea to help manage his business while he recuperated. He promised to pay my expenses and a small fee.

While I earned him a profit, my own bills kept mounting. My wife and I had a new home, and expenses were smothering me. My friend was still in the hospital, and I couldn't ask him to rescue me. But I was in danger of losing my home.

One rainy night as I rode the bus home, I decided to say the rosary. My mother had been dedicated to Our Lady through that prayer and always believed it worked. I was praying the Glorious Mysteries and decided to ask the Blessed Mother for help out of our desperate predicament.

That same night, I received a call from an international architectural engineering and construction firm offering a consulting assignment at $150 a day, plus expenses—very good money in those days. The project was successful, and I ended up working for that fine firm for the next 15 years.

I still pray the rosary every day.

—John, St. James, New York

Rainbows from Mary

My son Rick was in the wrong place at the wrong time. It nearly cost him his life.

There was a fight after a bachelor party he attended. He ended up getting punched in the head and slammed into the pavement. It wasn't even Rick's party—he is married with three children. There had been a lot of drinking going on, but my son had not had anything to drink because his company was sending him to school later that day. At the hospital, where he was rushed, his blood-alcohol level was zero.

The injury put Rick in a coma with severe brain damage. As soon as we heard, everyone began to pray for him. As the week drew on, we sat at his bedside talking to him, hoping he would hear us and awaken.

On Saturday, which was the day before the anniversary of Rick's grandfather's death, we re-doubled our prayers for God not to take two family members on the same date. But Rick remained in a coma.

Sunday dawned gray and ugly. I looked up to heaven and prayed to Mary, beseeching her as a mother to help me get my son back. In the late afternoon, I was talking with a friend on the phone when I looked out the window and saw the most beautiful rainbow through the trees in my yard. It was prettier than diamonds and glittered like a Christmas card.

Suddenly I felt such a peace. I called my daughter and told her Rick would be all right; the Blessed Mother had sent me a sign.

The next morning, when I got out my rosary to pray, it seemed to sparkle in the same way that the rainbow had. Within days, my son awoke from his coma. He had to undergo some rehabilitation but learned again how to walk and feed himself. Today, he still has some short-term memory problems, but otherwise he's okay.

I know I saw a miracle in that crystal rainbow.

Dorothy, Joliet, Illinois

Prayer of Consecration to Mary

O you, who are so deeply and maternally bound to the Church, preceding the whole People of God along the way of faith, hope and charity, embrace all who are on the way, pilgrims through temporal life towards eternal destinies, with that love which the Divine Redeemer himself, your Son, poured into your heart from the Cross. Be the Mother of all our earthly lives, even when they become tortuous, in order that we may all find ourselves, in the end, in that large community which your Son called the fold, offering his life for it as the Good Shepherd.

— *Pope John Paul II*

Virgin Most Powerful

*Mary, Mother of God and
Virgin Most Powerful,
you give to those who seek you
comfort, consolation and welcome.*

*But of all your many gifts,
most of all you bless us
with the power of one
who loved our Lord
both as savior and as son.*

*Help us to know
that you are with us always.*

*We ask this through Jesus,
your Son, our Lord.
Amen.*

Miracle in the Rain

Driving to Mass one Sunday morning, the sky shattered and a thunderstorm burst upon us. The sun was nowhere to be seen.

My wife, Kathy, and I and our six daughters neared the church with no sign of a letup in the pounding storm. I suggested the family pray together a *Hail, Mary* with the intention that the rain stop so we could get to Mass on time and remain dry at the same time.

I am not in the habit of putting God to the test; I reasoned, however, that this was a good intention. Besides, I remembered the Blessed Virgin Mary's promise to Christians that: *"You shall receive all you ask of me by the recitation of the rosary."* And I also recalled Jesus' promises, including the one from the Gospel of John: *"I will do whatever you ask in my name, so that the Father may be glorified in the Son"* *(John 14:13).*

So, with an eye on the storm encircling us, we prayed.

It was still pouring as we pulled into the church parking lot. Kathy asked me to drop off her and the children before parking the car. She said I would get wet but most of the family would stay dry.

She may get angry at me for telling this story, but it's the truth. I suggested they stay in the car until

I parked. I assured her that our prayer would be answered and the rain would cease. I had absolute faith.

I was remembering the words of Jesus that faith could move mountains. Surely faith could stop a storm, couldn't it?

But Kathy insisted, so I pulled up to near the door. She, along with our oldest daughter and the baby, made for the church. They got soaked.

As soon as I pulled into a parking space, though, the rain suddenly let up and the sun broke through the clouds. It was amazing; only moments before the sky had been black. The four other children and I strolled into the church—on time and completely dry!

Scant minutes later, the skies reopened and the thunder, lightning and rain carried on as horribly as before. It even knocked out the power to the church. We finished Mass by candlelight.

Some may say this was all a coincidence. Perhaps it is, but when you consider our prayer I believe it truly was a miracle. It not only kept us dry, but helped with our faith. I have gone from being a lukewarm Catholic to attending daily Mass and praying the rosary every day. I thank Jesus and the Queen of the Rosary for this miracle.

—Jim, Frankfort, Illinois

The Power of Prayer

I have always believed in the power of prayer. I pray the rosary daily. I began after becoming familiar with the recent reported appearances of the Blessed Mother around the world. I was moved by Mary's message that we should pray, pray, pray. I was in a very low period of my life. Even with daily prayer, I felt such an emptiness. I didn't think Our Lady or Jesus were hearing me. I felt very alone.

I asked the Blessed Mother to give me a sign that she and Jesus had not deserted me. I prayed, "Dear Mary, if you are really with me, please turn my rosary to gold."

Each evening I made this request, but I soon realized how ludicrous it was. I became angry with myself. I have never required such assurances to deepen my faith. In the past when my faith seemed lessened or was challenged, I would place it all in God's hands and allow his will to be done. Why did I need a sign now?

Christmas arrived. My in-laws gave me a new rosary. When I took it out of the wrapping and looked at it, it was beautiful. The crucifix was made from interlocking Xs and the beads appeared to be marbleized pebbles.

After we returned home and settled in for the night, I sat down to pray my new rosary. As I began the Creed, I suddenly noticed I was holding a golden rosary. It seemed different than when I had unwrapped it.

Chills ran down my spine and tears came to my eyes. I shouted, "Oh, my God," and called for my husband. I said, "Jim, my new rosary; it's a gold one!" He replied, "Yeah, it is. Don't you like it?" When I told him about how I had prayed to Mary two months earlier and how that prayer had now been answered, he too had tears in his eyes.

When I told my mother-in-law the story of my small miracle, she said, "Bob (my father-in-law) wanted me to get you a silver rosary, but I kept going back to the gold one. It looked like it belonged to you."

I have told this story to many people. Some say, "It was just a coincidence." My reply is always that it was my small miracle from the Blessed Mother. She conveyed to me two very strong messages. First, when we feel abandoned, Our Lady and Jesus are still near us. Second, she kept her promise to all Christians: *"You shall receive all you ask of me by the recitation of the rosary."*

—Gina, Joliet, Illinois

From Disneyland to Our Lady

It might seem strange, but we had an experience with the Blessed Mother on the way back from Disneyland. It happened like this.

My mother and I, along with my daughter and niece, were returning from a visit to the Magic Kingdom. We stopped in Santa Maria, California, to see the spot where people said Blessed Mary was asking that a "cross of peace" be built overlooking a freeway. We discovered about 70 people already there, all praying the rosary.

The presence of God was so powerful that I told our group that we couldn't go on until we too had prayed. So we gathered together, held hands, and prayed and prayed.

While we were praying, I asked for a healing of my niece, who had such severe deformity that doctors told her even surgery would be unlikely to help. Well, exactly a year to the week later, she underwent that surgery. Correction was 100 percent; even the doctors told her that was extremely rare.

—Sherry, Chadron, Nebraska

The Room Was Spinning

Several years ago I was diagnosed with Meniere's Disease, a middle-ear affliction that left me dizzy and suffering from vertigo for hours at a time. It was horrible.

One evening at bedtime, I had such a severe attack that when I finally awoke in the morning the room was still spinning. It was so bad I couldn't get out of the bed. Figuring the next few hours were going to be useless, I asked my husband to hand me a rosary. I could at least pray a decade or so and make the time pass.

As soon as I touched my rosary, the room stopped spinning. Though I still have a ringing in my left ear, I have not had an attack of vertigo since.

—Marie, Portland, Oregon

A Prayer to Mary for Peace

Mother of the Prince of Peace, Mediatrix
between rebellious humans and the merciful
God, you are the dawn of peace shining in
the darkness of a world out of joint; you
never cease to implore your Son for peace,
although his hour is not yet come; you
always intervene on behalf of sorrowing
humanity in the hour of danger; you are the
mother of many orphans and our advocate in
this tremendous catastrophe.

Hear our prayers.

—Pope Benedict XV

Virgin Most Merciful

Mary, Mother of God
and Virgin Most Merciful,
we come to you at every turn of our lives,
seeking your comfort and your mercy.

You are always there for us
no matter what our need or pain.

Plead with us to Jesus,
face the Father with our hurts and hope.

We ask this through Jesus,
your Son, our Lord.
Amen.

Angels, Icons, Tears and Knees

When my sister was in a nursing home, I drove the tortuous 75-mile trip twice a week to see her. This meant a 150-mile round trip journey through winter weather that was often very bad.

The worst trip of all was on one pitch black, raining and blowing night. Of course I started praying, telling God all about it. Then he showed me a band of pink angels around my car. So I settled back, started the engine, and drove home without a bit of trouble! I know these angels are with me still.

That was just one of the experiences that let me know that God cares. Here's another. Several years ago, the icon of the Blessed Mother at the Albanian Orthodox Church in my city began weeping. I watched as one of the priests was blessing a young boy with the Blessed Mother's tears. I went right over and asked for a healing too.

The priest looked at me and said, "Why? You look pretty healthy to me."

I said, "Father, it's my knees." I had to sit on the edge of the pew instead of kneeling properly.

The priest looked me over and said, "We don't do knees." But he did anoint my forehead, chin and hands.

Yet I haven't had a minute's trouble with my knees ever since. I can kneel just fine.

—Loretta, Chicago, Illinois

Prayers and Paralysis

Our beautiful daughter, Victoria, is a blessed miracle. When she was 11 months old, she developed a fever. The doctor said it was just an ear infection, but it wasn't. The fever spiked, and she began to have seizures. After the ambulance rushed her to the hospital, we noticed that she wasn't moving one side of her body.

At first, the doctor thought the paralysis was just a temporary reaction to the high fever, but a spinal tap was positive for meningitis. He said it was the worst case he'd ever seen. Now he wasn't even sure she'd live. And if Victoria by some miracle did survive, he said, she would surely suffer brain damage. They moved our beautiful little girl to intensive care, hooking her up with many wires and machines to help keep her alive.

That night, my husband I prayed in the hospital chapel that Victoria would live and that we would be able to deal with her brain damage. Later, in her room, I rocked my very sick little girl, repeating Our Lady's rosary over and over.

Two days later, they removed Victoria from the ICU. She was responding extraordinarily well to medication. The doctor said she didn't seem to have suffered brain damage after all, though she would likely turn out to be a slow student.

Today our daughter is a delightful young lady—
and a straight-A student!

God answered our prayers, and more.

—Stella, Katy, Texas

Lumps and Lourdes

A few years ago I found a lump in the corner of my eye.

The doctor told me it would probably need surgery, but we compromised on trying hot compresses on the eye first. For several weeks, nothing happened. Then I used some water that had come from Lourdes.

At my next appointment, the doctor could find no sign of the infection. I was healed. I know it was the Lourdes water that did it.

—Mary, Albany, New York

Peace Is Its Own Cure

Several years ago, I was diagnosed with a connective-tissue disease called dermatomyositis. It weakens the muscles, and there is no cure. It can even be fatal if it attacks internal organs.

After a year and a half of trying to find someone or something to blame for this malady, I knew I had to find some peace within myself. I could not go on living such a bitter, miserable life.

This was back in 1988. I began hearing about the place called Medjugorje. Everywhere I turned, there was Medjugorje—on the news, in magazines, people talking about it. I knew I had to go. We had no money for such a trip, so we borrowed it. My husband was hoping for a miraculous recovery for me, but I went for another reason: peace of mind and peace with God.

When we arrived in Yugoslavia (as it was named then), I expected the sun to begin dancing, like it did at Fatima. It didn't. I expected my rosary to turn instantly to gold. It didn't. I was pretty disappointed.

Mass in the Church of St. James was a powerful experience; I was so touched. We were determined to climb Cross Mountain, even though I was using a cane at the time. We went in late afternoon, when it would be cooler.

I never knew the terrain would be so rocky. My husband went up first, pulling me up after him. It was four hours of sheer torture. About halfway up I saw an old man coming down, being helped by two older women. If they could make it, so could I, I thought.

When we finally reached the top, it was awesome, serene. We stayed awhile and prayed. On the summit, we noticed a dog that had come wandering out of the brush limping from a thorn in his paw. My husband took out the thorn and we started down. It was dark but we had a small flashlight. We thought going down would be easier; it wasn't; and there was no way my husband could carry me. We became lost. The small flashlight was useless.

Suddenly, the dog from the summit was there and began to lead us. We followed that mutt all the way down. At the bottom, the dog just disappeared back into the brush.

That was a miracle, all right, but the biggest miracle was the inner peace I received. I knew I could go on with a positive attitude. This horrible disease was not something to blame on God, it was a blessing in disguise; I became a better person because of it.

I've encouraged several members of my family to pray the rosary regularly. When you become an apostle of Mary, she touches your life in ways you never thought possible.

—Cathy, Winfield, Illinois

A Prayer to Mary for Christian Unity

O you who are the first Handmaid of the unity of the Body of Christ, help us. Help all the faithful who feel so painfully the drama of the divisions of Christianity seek with constancy the way to the perfect unity of the Body of Christ by means of unconditional faithfulness to the Spirit of Truth and Love, which was given to us by your Son at the cost of the Cross and of death.

—Pope John Paul II

Mystical Rose

Mother Mary,
throughout centuries of devotion,
roses have been your symbol.

They recall for us the blossom
of your love, the freshness of your life,
and your role in bringing newness
to all things.

Help us when we
see, smell and enjoy
the gentle softness of a rose,
to understand how close you are to us.

We ask this through Jesus,
your Son, our Lord.
Amen.

The Miracles of the Roses

Roses always remind me of Mary, since they are her flower. And Mary, of course, always reminds me of miracles—my miracles, at least. One year on August 15, the Feast of the Assumption, I asked my husband to move a large flat rock to the shrine to Our Lady in our yard. I wanted to elevate her statue a little higher.

During a violent windstorm earlier that summer, a branch from a nearby rosebush had been knocked over right in front of her statue. There was a single rose on the branch, so I had left it there. It was flat on the ground, and I was certain it would die soon.

The day after we raised Mary's statue, however, instead of a single rose on that forlorn branch, there were seven. And another new bud! There were more blossoms on that wounded branch than on all the other rose bushes in my garden. To me this was a sign of God's love through Mary. And it's why to this day I keep three silk roses in a vase by a figure of the Risen Christ in my dining room.

That crucifix and the three roses are part of another miracle. Early one morning, after a sleepless night, I felt strange. I am a diabetic and felt like I was having an insulin reaction. I tested my blood, though, and it was okay. Still, it had been several hours since I had eaten, so I decided to fix myself something.

I remember I was admiring the white vase and three red silk roses by the crucifix. Above them in large gold print are the words from St. Paul, *"I can do all things through him who strengthens me" (Philippians 4:13).* As I was getting my food, I must have slipped into a deep diabetic shock. I recall rising to near-consciousness several times before falling even deeper. The first time, I recognized my medication on the floor. The next time, I saw my tray of food with coffee spilled all over it. The third time, I remember feeling for my eyeglasses. I must have put them on when I turned and focused on the roses and the line from Scripture. Even though I was semiconscious, that saying was firmly planted in my mind.

It had to have been the power of the Holy Spirit that roused me, nearly two hours into this dangerous state, to fumble with the phone and call the home of one of my high school religion students who lived across the street. I remember pushing the buttons and heard a voice. "I need help," I mumbled.

My neighbors were able to get some orange juice into me, but I kept slipping away. It took paramedics, an ambulance, and several hours in the hospital before I finally was brought around.

Somehow Mary's roses and the crucifix and the words, "I can do all things through him who strengthens me," helped me make that call. It had to have been a miracle.

—Rosalie, Whitehall, Illinois

The Unquenchable Golden Rose

The power of a small, golden rose is undeniable; it reminds me of the power of God.

During a pilgrimage to the Shrine of Mary in Fatima, Portugal, my husband and I placed a golden artificial rose at the foot of the Virgin's statue in the Chapel of Apparitions. During the day, we watched hundreds of pilgrims place bouquets in the same area. Our little golden rose was buried beneath a mountain of fresh flowers.

Later, we returned to the chapel. Caretakers had moved all the bouquets to the back of the chapel. But our little golden rose was right where we had left it. We were both surprised and pleased.

After supper, we returned again to participate in the chapel's procession in honor of Our Lady of Fatima. Once again, our little rose was overwhelmed by fresh flowers. We felt certain that this time it would be lost.

The following day, before we left for home, we made one last visit to the chapel to attend Mass. To our utter amazement, the little golden rose was still there. How could that happen, we wondered?

After Mass, I went to the shrine to pray and leave a picture of our family and a message to the Virgin on one of the altars. My husband, however, stayed behind in the chapel and watched as the caretakers tidied up near the statue. Several times they moved our golden rose around, but then one of the caretakers looked at it, picked it up, and brought it to the chapel altar.

Not only did our little golden rose survive the avalanche of fresh flowers, but it ended up in the most honored place of all.

—Catherine, Spring, Texas

Surviving the Storm

The storm awakened us before dawn. The clatter of the hailstones—some as large as tennis balls—was deafening. After 15 minutes, the ground was white and the damage was frightening.

The August storm stripped bare our trees and destroyed the vegetable and perennial flower garden I'd tended for nearly 50 years. Only the carrots and potatoes, safe below ground, survived. There was more than $25,000 damage to our roof, windows, screens, and a metal shed. We were fortunate that no one was hurt in the early-morning battering.

But here was the miracle: the only flowers not damaged by the pelting iceballs were those I planted in front of our statue of the Blessed Virgin Mary. The little shrine had some paint chipped off, but no other damage.

Neighbors stopped by and were amazed that those flowers were spared. No one can persuade me that Our Lady didn't intercede to save them.

—Evelyn, New Prague, Minnesota

The Everlasting Roses

The miracle I am telling about happened in England many years ago, but I have a personal connection to it, so I know it's true.

In May 1947, near London, a parish crowned a statue of Mary with a wreath of yellow roses. That wreath remained fresh all year, even until the following spring when another was placed upon the first. Both then remained fresh.

I saw a report of this phenomenon in the movie newsreels. I corresponded with the parish priest for a long time, until he retired. He sent me several photographs of the miracle as it happened.

—Chester, Westchester, Illinois

Affirmation of Mary's Place of Honor

I do not hesitate to affirm that God effected every liberation and granted every pardon solely out of reverence and love for the Blessed Maiden. In virtue of this reverence and love, God predestined her, foreordaining from all eternity that she be honored before all his other works.

—St. Bernadine of Siena

Mary, Help of Christians

Mother Mary,
to whom do people cling
when trouble comes?
They fly to their mother, of course,
for protection.

You are the Mother of the Church,
the Mother of Jesus,
the Mother of God.
Indeed, you are the Mother of us all.

To you we cling when danger threatens,
to your side in prayer we flee.
Mary, Help of Christians everywhere,
help us.

We ask this through Jesus,
your Son, our Lord.
Amen.

The Not-So-Missing Bead

When oil prices tumbled in the late 1980s, the economy of Houston went down too. My husband's dental practice was suffering terribly, and our home was being repossessed. It was bad news on top of tragedy—several years earlier, our two teenaged daughters had been killed in a car crash. I still kept praying, but I was becoming depressed.

My prayers for the success of my husband's business and to sell our home before we lost it were not being heard. Or so I feared.

One evening, I said to my husband, "I don't think I believe in the Communion of Saints anymore. I'm really angry because we've received no help from my prayers."

We had gone to bed that night, but my husband was upset over our financial situation. He awakened and phoned his sister for consolation. It didn't seem to ease his anxiety, so he turned on the TV. Some preacher was shrieking his message on a late-night religion channel. It was so irritating that I told my husband, "You can sit there and listen to that high-volume sermon if you want, or you can come with me. I'm going to pray the rosary."

He joined me. As we prayed, my fingers reach the spot on my rosary—the beginning of the final decade—where a bead has been missing for 35 years. It was there! I hurried to finish the prayers and checked in a bright light. I was amazed; I had used the rosary only two days earlier, but now it was complete.

I was so overcome with a feeling of the presence of the Holy Spirit that I wept uncontrollably. I knew then, beyond a shadow of a doubt, that my prayers had been heard, that Our Blessed Mother, Jesus, and even our daughters were telling me to keep praying and not to worry.

We were able to sell our property, and in the years since that experience my husband's practice has increased. Now we are ready to buy another home.

I know now that Mary and Jesus love us and that we should never give up praying. Our prayers may not always be answered when and how we want them to be, but they will be answered.

Now when things get me down, I think about my rosary miracle and feel very close to God. I know he will always take care of me.

—Mrs. F., Houston, Texas

A Grandmother's Vision

Elizabeth Kennedy Tighe—my grandmother Lizzie—
was among the three little girls who witnessed the
appearance of Our Blessed Lady in the little town of
Knock, County Mayo, Ireland, in 1879. Mary—
accompanied by St. Joseph, St. John, and angels—
appeared at the church of St. John the Baptist, and
today the spot is the national Irish Shrine to Our
Lady, visited by hundreds of thousands of pilgrims
each year. The Church refers to their vision as Our
Lady of Knock.

Lizzie emigrated with her parents to Bayonne,
New Jersey, where her father worked as a butcher.
In her adopted country, Lizzie married Patrick Joseph Tighe. Together they raised nine children. She
died in 1956 at the age of 56.

Her story—and her adamant devotion to
Mary—has been a constant source of strength to me
and to my faith. All my life I have asked for Our
Blessed Lady's help in small matters and in larger
ones. I cannot recall ever having been refused.

—Jackie, Wilmington, Delaware

Cooking with God

I always yearned to be part of the visions of Mary, but it seemed an impossible dream; they all happened so far away.

One time I entered a cooking contest, hoping to win enough money to fund a pilgrimage. Even my recipe was inspired by the Holy Spirit—"Beef Simply Divine" I called it. And it earned me a spot as a finalist in the New York State cook-offs.

Several days before the final contest, I went on a retreat. During Mass, I prayed aloud for help, explaining that if I won I would be able to make my long-desired pilgrimage. It seemed like only minutes later that a sweet-faced woman came over to me. She said she had followed the Lord's urging to attend this particular retreat. She told me she knew she would be led to the person God intended. Then she pressed $1,000 into my surprised hands. I was going; I was going on a pilgrimage! But then I learned the trip would cost $1,280. Well, you guessed it. The cook-offs came, and I won second prize—$280.

A few weeks later I was airborne. It was incredible. I found Mary waiting for me with open arms. That journey lives on in my heart, and I will yearn for the Blessed Mother until I meet her and Jesus in eternity.

—Rose Mary, Stony Brook, New York

Invocation to Mary

From every corner of the earth—from the majestic churches and the humble chapels; from the mansions of the rich as well as from the huts of the poor; from wherever dwells a faithful soul; from the bloodstained battle-fields and war-swept seas—may this pious and ardent invocation arise to Mary, the Mother of Mercy, who is all-powerful in grace!

To Mary may be brought each anguished cry of mothers and wives, each tear of innocent children, each longing of generous hearts! May her loving and most merciful solicitude be moved to obtain for this convulsed world the peace so greatly desired! And may the ages yet to come remember the efficacy of Mary's intercession and the greatness of her blessings to her suppliants!

—Pope Benedict XV

Queen of Angels

Mary, Mother of Our Lord
and Queen of Angels,
you know the joys, fears and pains
of motherhood.

With our hearts we dedicate to you,
Mother of Mothers,
the angels in our lives,
those children given us by God.

Help us, Mother of Mothers,
to always see in them
the hope of the future.

We ask this through Jesus,
your Son, our Lord.
Amen.

With a Half-Ounce to Spare

My husband and I were ecstatic when our youngest daughter told us we were to be grandparents. We could hardly contain ourselves after seeing this little person through a doctor's sonogram.

But our joy quickly turned to fear when our daughter went into labor very early. Though the doctors were able to stop the contractions in time, our family was suddenly faced with the possibility of dealing with a very premature baby.

I immediately contacted our church to ask for prayers. The parish secretary suggested that my prayers be directed toward the Blessed Mother. She, I was told, would certainly understand our concern.

As a convert to Catholicism, I had a difficult time understanding the role of Mary in the Church and was uncomfortable with this sort of intercessory prayer. Desperate for a miracle, however, I began to talk each day with Mary, asking her to intercede with the Lord and protect our daughter and her unborn child.

As the weeks passed, I began to feel a strange sense of peace, and when the birth became imminent I grew bolder and quite specific in my daily conversations with Mary. I prayed that the baby would weigh at least four pounds.

Our grandson was born nine weeks early. Nurses were as overjoyed as we were, because he breathed on his own right from birth. Our daughter was able to bring him home only three weeks later.

How do I know this was a miracle? The little guy weighed four pounds and one-half ounce—a little extra from Our Lady for good measure! Then our daughter, who did not know of my talks with Mary, told me his name would be Joseph.

God truly touched our lives, and we are blessed.

—Karlyn, Bangor, Maine

Naming a Miracle

When my husband and I were first married, we hoped for children. After three years, we were still hoping, but we were also praying. I promised the Blessed Mother that if I would only have a little girl, I would name her Elizabeth Ann or Mary Elizabeth.

When I still failed to conceive, we filed for adoption, still praying to Mary.

One day the phone rang. It was the Catholic agency. They had a little girl for us. Her name was Elizabeth Ann. I didn't answer. I couldn't. I was in shock. The nun on the other end of the line was perplexed by my silence. She quickly said that if we didn't like the name we could always change it. I stammered out the story of my promise to Mary. She, quite naturally, was amazed. But there's more.

A year later, we sought to adopt another child, this time a boy. The name we liked was Michael Brian. There had been a statue of St. Michael the Archangel on the grounds of the grade school I had attended, and I prayed often to St. Michael. I still do. When we were told a baby boy was available, we were told his name was Michael Bryant.

Needless to say, my husband and I never doubt the power of prayer.

—Rosemary, Smithtown, New York

Miracle Increases Faith, Hope, Love

My husband and I struggled through the pains of infertility for many years. It took a long time before we could become open to the idea of adoption, but after a miscarriage we were able to consider it seriously. We realized it was less important for us where the baby came from; we just wanted a child to love.

But even that road was rough and potholed, because our attempts to adopt were stalled for various reasons. We continued hoping I would get pregnant naturally. We even made a pilgrimage to Medjugorje, hoping, perhaps, that a child might be conceived in that holy place. What a glorious thought!

Eight months after our pilgrimage, though, there still was no baby in sight from pregnancy or adoption, and I was so depressed. I couldn't even answer the phone because I'd burst into tears whenever someone said, "How are you?"

I prayed, asking for a sign on March 25—feast of the Annunciation of Our Lord and just nine months after our hopeful time at Mary's shrine— whether or not we were ever going to have a baby. Just a week later, I received a phone call from a social worker who said there was a baby available who was actually due on March 25. I didn't know if this was the answer to my prayer, but bells were ringing in my head and my heart was pounding.

The end of this chapter of our miracle story is that our beautiful son, Andrew, was given to us nine months after our pilgrimage. This miracle—with all the subtle signs of God's control—has not only given us a treasured child but also increased our faith, hope, love and joy in God's presence in our lives.

—Madeleine, Richland, Washington

A Prayer of Consecration of the Human Family to Mary

O Mother of All Peoples, you know all their sufferings and their hopes. You feel in a motherly way all the struggles between good and evil, between light and darkness that shakes the world. Accept our cry addressed to the Holy Spirit directly to your heart and embrace with the love of the Mother and the Handmaid of the Lord the peoples who await this embrace the most, and likewise the peoples whose consecration you, too, are particularly awaiting.

Take under your motherly protection the whole human family which we consecrate to you, O Mother, with affectionate rapture. May the time of peace and freedom, the time of truth, justice and hope, approach for everyone.

—*Pope John Paul II*

Traditional Marian Prayers

Prayers to Mary, especially the recitation of the rosary, are a strong part of the Christian tradition. Over the centuries, many beautiful formal prayers to Our Lady have been composed and repeated all over the world. What follows are but a few of the more popular Marian prayers.

Hail, Mary

Hail, Mary, full of grace, the Lord is with you.

Blessed are you among women and blessed is the fruit of your womb, Jesus.

Holy Mary, Mother of God, pray for us sinners, now and at the hour of our death.

Amen.

Hail, Holy Queen

Hail, Holy Queen, Mother of Mercy, hail our life, our sweetness, and our hope.

To you we cry, poor banished children of Eve.

To you we send up our sighs, mourning and weeping in this valley of tears.

Turn then, most gracious advocate, your eyes of mercy toward us.

And after this our exile show us unto the blessed fruit of your womb, Jesus.

O clement, O loving, O sweet Virgin Mary.

Amen.

Mary, Seat of Wisdom

O happy Virgin, you gave birth to the
Lord; O blessed Seat of Wisdom, you
cradle in our hearts the spirit of your
Son, Jesus Christ.

Amen.

The Memorare

Remember, O most gracious Virgin Mary, that never was it known that anyone who fled to your protection, implored your help, or sought your intercession was left unaided.

Inspired by this confidence, I fly to you, O Virgin of virgins, my Mother; to you I come, before you I stand, sinful and sorrowful.

O Mother of the Word Incarnate, despise not my petitions, but in your mercy hear and answer me.

Amen.

Queen of Heaven

Queen of Heaven, rejoice, alleluia: for he whom you merited to bear, alleluia, has risen as he said, alleluia.

Pray for us to God, alleluia.

Amen.

Prayer for Forgiveness

I confess to Almighty God, and to you, my brothers and sisters, that I have sinned through my own fault in my thoughts and in my words, in what I have done, and in what I have failed to do.

I ask blessed Mary, ever virgin, all the angels and saints, and you, my brothers and sisters, to pray for me to the Lord our God.

Amen.

The Magnificat

My soul proclaims the greatness of the Lord, my spirit rejoices in God my Savior, for he has looked with favor upon his lowly handmaiden.

From this day forward all generations will call me blessed.

The Almighty has done great things for me, and holy is his name.

Amen.

Mary, Help of Christians

Mary, powerful Virgin, you are the mighty and glorious protector of the Church.

You are the marvelous help of Christians.

You are awe-inspiring as an army in battle array.

You eliminated heresy in the world.

Amid our anguish, struggle and distress, defend us from the power of the enemy, and at the hour of our death receive our soul into heaven.

Amen.

Mary's Feast Days

We can honor Mary every day, but the Church marks official Marian devotions often throughout the year. The Christian calendar provides for 15 "Mary Days" or feast days when an event in her life or a connection to the saving power of her Son, Jesus, is re-called. These days are listed here.

Mary, the Mother of God

The title, Mother of God, granted to Mary by the Council of Ephesus in 431, earns this Marian feast day the honor of being the oldest in her honor. This feast is celebrated on January 1.

Our Lady of Lourdes

This feast is celebrated on February 11, the day the first apparition of Mary appeared in 1858 to a 14-year-old French girl named Bernadette Soubirous, who would come to known as St. Bernadette. The appearances of the Blessed Mother to Bernadette—18 in all—were officially recognized by the Church only a few year later. The waters from the chapel in Lourdes have been credited since then with many healings. Some officially acknowledged appearances of the Blessed Mother—such as the one at Fatima in Portugal—are celebrated as feasts in other countries but not in the United States.

Annunciation of Our Lord

The celebration on March 25 marks the conception of Jesus by the Holy Spirit in Mary's womb. As such, it is a feast of Jesus, though we also acknowledge Mary for her undeniably essential role.

The Visitation

Mary's cousin Elizabeth, long without child but pregnant with John the Baptizer, greeted Mary with the immortal words, "Blessed are you among women, and blessed is the fruit of your womb," which we pray in the *Hail, Mary*. It was in response to this that Mary responded, "My soul magnifies the Lord," which is the beginning of her prayer called the Magnificat. We celebrate this scene each May 31.

The Immaculate Heart of Mary

The celebration of this feast occurs on various days in June, dependent on the date of Easter. It was proclaimed in 1944 by Pope Pius XII in honor of Mary's sinlessness.

Our Lady of Mt. Carmel

The Carmelites, by ancient tradition, mark July 16 as the date when the brown scapular was given in an appearance by Mary to St. Simon Stock. It was, she is to have told him, a sign of her love.

Dedication of St. Mary Major

Mary's preeminent role as Mother of the Church is linked to this feast day, celebrated on August 5. The ancient Basilica of St. Mary Major in Rome is named for her.

The Assumption

In 1950, Pope Pius XII defined the dogma of the Assumption, stating that upon her death Mary was assumed bodily into heaven. However, the date of August 15 honoring her death was first marked as early as the seventh century.

The Queenship of Mary

Pope Pius XII, who was deeply devoted to the Blessed Mother, authorized the celebration of the Queenship of Mary in 1954 following the establishment of the Feast of Christ the King. Mary, as the first saint, also is considered Queen of All Saints, and we celebrate this feast on August 22.

Our Lady of Sorrows

September 8 marks a remembrance of Mary's sorrows as a widow and a mother whose son was taken from her.

Our Lady of the Rosary

The entire month of October is dedicated by the Church to the rosary, the uniquely Marian prayer. The feast day is October 7.

Presentation of Mary in the Temple

There is no biblical record of such an event actually taking place. Rather, since it was a Jewish custom to bring all children to the Temple soon after birth for the acknowledgment of the community, the Church recognizes that Mary, too, would have been presented. It celebrates her presentation on November 21.

The Immaculate Conception

Since Mary was chosen by God to bear Jesus in her womb, she must certainly have herself been born sinless. This is the understanding behind the dogma of Mary's Immaculate Conception, defined in 1854 by Pope Pius IX. Mary, as the Immaculate Conception, is the patroness of the United States, and this special relationship is celebrated on December 8.

Our Lady of Guadalupe

In 1531, the Virgin Mary appeared to a Mexican peasant, Juan Diego. This event has become one of great reverence, especially among Hispanics. Our Lady of Guadalupe Basilica in Mexico City is a destination of many pilgrims each year. She is honored on December 12 as the Patroness of the Americas.

An Invitation to Share Miracles

More than 2,000 people have already responded to the following invitation to tell their stories of miracles in their lives. It is a simple request placed in newspapers and church bulletins that asks:

Do you know a small miracle? I believe most people do, if they really think about it. Not necessarily a major league miracle like water turning into wine or the Red Sea parting, just the everyday sort that lets us know God is alive and well—a moment when God touches our lives. I'm inviting people from all over to share their small miracles. It might be something that seems unimportant—except to you—perhaps a healing, an insight, an event or even an opportunity. Please share them with me.

Do you have a small miracle story? Did God, Our Lady or one of the saints touch your life in a special way? Please add your testament to those of many others by sending it to:

Tom Sheridan
Small Miracles
Post Office Box 3003-120
Naperville, IL 60566

About the Author

Tom Sheridan is the editor and general manager of New World Publications of the Archdiocese of Chicago. He is a former columnist and member of the editorial board of the *Chicago Sun-Times* and the author of several books, including *Small Miracles: Extraordinary Stories of Ordinary People Touched by God*, *The Gift of Godparents* and *The Gift of Baptism*. Mr. Sheridan is a permanent deacon in the Catholic Church and a husband, father and grandfather.

Also Available from ACTA Publications

The Rosary. A complete recitation of all 15 mysteries of the Rosary, with original music and meditations. (90-minute audio cassette, $9.95; compact disc, $12.95; video, $19.95)

Rosary Novenas to Our Lady. The classic "little blue book" by Charles V. Lacey on how to pray the rosary novena, with a reflection for each mystery. (48-page booklet, $4.95)

Our Mother of Perpetual Help Novena. Novena prayers, hymns and an inspiring message about devotion to Our Mother of Perpetual Help. (45-minute audio cassette with prayer booklet, $8.95)

The Novenas with Music. Five popular novenas, including the Novena to Our Lady of Perpetual Help, with beautiful choral and orchestral music. (30-minute audio cassette, $8.95)

The Litanies with Music. Five popular litanies, including the Litany of Our Lady of Loretto, with beautiful choral and orchestral music. (30-minute audio cassette, $8.95)

The Stations of the Cross. The traditional Way of the Cross, with original music and meditations. (45-minute audio cassette, $8.95; compact disc, $12.95; video, $19.95)

**Available from bookstores or
by calling 800-397-2282.**